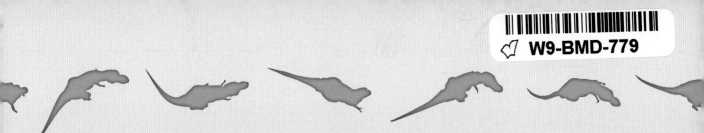

The Age of Dinosaurs

Meet PACHYCEPHALOSAURUS

Written by Henley Miller

Illustrations by Leonello Calvetti and Luca Massini

Cavendish Square

New York

Published in 2014 by Cavendish Square Publishing, LLC
303 Park Avenue South, Suite 1247, New York, NY 10010

Copyright © 2014 by Cavendish Square Publishing, LLC

First Edition

CPSIA Compliance Information: Batch #WW14CSQ

All websites were available and accurate when this book was sent to press.

Library of Congress Cataloging-in-Publication Data

Miller, Henley.
Meet pachycephalosaurus / by Henley Miller.
p. cm. — (The age of dinosaurs)
Includes index.
ISBN 978-1-62712-616-8 (hardcover) ISBN 978-1-62712-617-5 (paperback) ISBN 978-1-62712-618-2 (ebook)
1. Pachycephalosaurus — Juvenile literature. I. Miller, Henley. II. Title.
QE862.S3 D35 2014
567.913—dc23

Editorial Director: Dean Miller
Art Director: Jeffrey Talbot
Designer: Joseph Macri
Photo Researcher: Julie Alissi, J8 Media
Production Manager: Jennifer Ryder-Talbot
Production Editor: Andrew Coddington

Illustration by Leonello Calvetti and Luca Massini.

The photographs in this book are used by permission and through the courtesy of: Debi Bishop/Vetta/Getty Images, 8; Gallo Images/the Agency Collection/Getty Images, 8; Ballista/Pachycephalosaurus skull/Own work/GNU Free Documentation License/Creative Commons Attribution-Share Alike 3.0 Unported license, 19, 20; Gerard Lacz Images/ SuperStock, 21.

Printed in the United States of America

CONTENTS

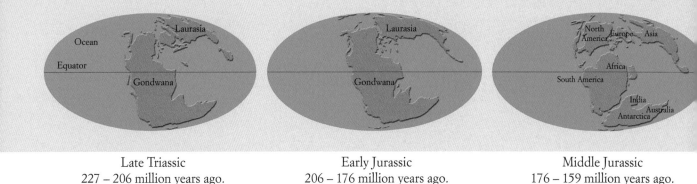

Late Triassic	Early Jurassic	Middle Jurassic
227 – 206 million years ago.	206 – 176 million years ago.	176 – 159 million years ago.

A CHANGING WORLD

Earth's long history began 4.6 billion years ago. Dinosaurs were among the most fascinating animals from Earth's long past.

The word "dinosaur" originates from the Greek words *deinos* and *sauros*, which together mean "fearfully great lizards."

To understand dinosaurs we need to understand geological time, the lifetime of our planet. Earth history is divided into eras, periods, epochs, and ages. The dinosaur era, called the Mesozoic Era, is divided in three periods: Triassic, which lasted 42 million years; Jurassic, 61 million years; and Cretaceous, 79 million years. Dinosaurs ruled the world for over 160 million years.

Late Jurassic	Early Cretaceous	Late Cretaceous
159 – 144 million years ago.	144 – 99 million years ago.	99 – 65 million years ago.

Man never met dinosaurs: they had disappeared nearly 65 million years before man's appearance on Earth.

The dinosaur world differed from our world. The climate was warmer, the continents were different, and grass did not even exist!

A VERY HARD HEAD

Pachycephalosaurus was probably a biped, moving on its two hind limbs, and is thought to have been more than 25 feet (7.6 m) long (since we have only the skull, this is only a guess). Scientists estimated that an adult Pachycephalosaurus weighed about 1–2 tons(0.9–1.8 t): a rather large animal.

The name derives from the Greek meaning "thick-headed lizard" and refers to the incredibly thick upper skull wall—all of 8 inches (20.3 cm). Actually, the principal feature of this dinosaur is the dome-shaped skull, which looked like a bald head.

FINDING PACHYCEPHALOSAURUS

Pachycephalosaurus lived in North America at the end of the Late Cretaceous Period, shortly before the large dinosaurs became extinct 65.5 million years ago. It lived in the semitropical coastal plain that stretched out between the Rocky Mountains to the west and the inner sea of the North American continent on the east. So far remains have been discovered in Wyoming, Montana, and South Dakota.

Montana

South Dakota

North America

This map shows part of North America in the Late Cretaceous Period. The dark brown patches indicate mountains and the red dots represent Pachycephalosaurus fossil discovery sites.

LITTLE HARD HEADS GROW UP

Pachycephalosaurus are still rather mysterious dinosaurs. We have no nests, eggs, or embryos of this species and so we know nothing about how they reproduced. It is probable that the skull domes of the babies were less developed, and that there were only traces of the ornamentation that distinguished the heads of the adults.

VEGETARIAN MEALS

Pachycephalosaurus teeth were rather small and triangular. This probably means that these dinosaurs were vegetarians, with a diet composed mainly of leaves, seeds, fruits, and buds of plants, although the young may also have eaten large insects.

Pachycephalosaurus' teeth were not as efficient as that of other dinosaur plant-eaters, such as Edmontosaurus and the Triceratops, which also lived in the coastal plains of North America.

BUTTING HEADS

The unbelievably strong head dome of Pachycephalosaurus
might have been used in fights to impress females. Two rivals
might have butted heads, like the mountain sheep of today.

FIGHTING WITH YOUR HEAD

The skull dome could also have served as defense against predators. This might have been possible for Pachycephalosaurus, but not for his smaller "cousins." According to some paleontologists, the different shapes of the skull dome served to identify the various species. They probably developed differently in males and females, helping to distinguish the sexes.

INSIDE PACHYCEPHALOSAURUS

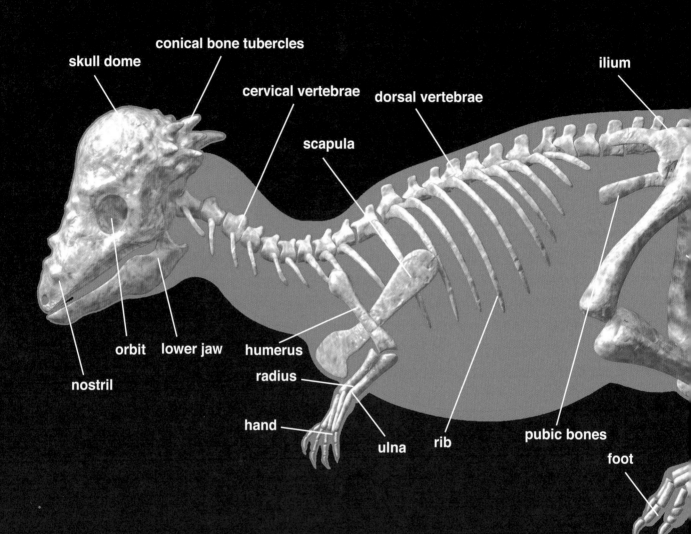

skull dome

conical bone tubercles

cervical vertebrae

dorsal vertebrae

ilium

scapula

orbit lower jaw humerus

nostril

radius

hand

ulna rib

pubic bones

foot

Actually the only part of Pachycephalosaurus we know is the large skull, which can measure up to two feet long. Reconstructions of the rest of the skeleton and the form of the body are based on fossils of other pachycephalosaurians, mostly Stegoceras, Homalocephale, and Goyocephale, who are all smaller in size. On this basis, our dinosaur must have been a biped, with a short robust neck, a bulky barrel-shaped body, and a heavy tail.

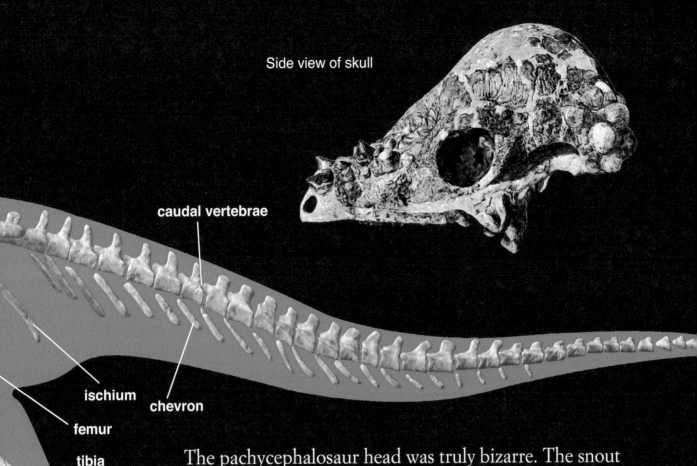

Side view of skull

caudal vertebrae

ischium

chevron

femur

tibia

thumb

The pachycephalosaur head was truly bizarre. The snout was relatively long and pointed with strong conical bone tubercles. More rounded tubercles were also on the back part of the skull and at the base of the large skull dome. The head dome, the distinctive feature of this dinosaur, was not hollow, like the skullcap of man which contains a large brain, but was all compact bone. The brain occupied only a small space at the base of the dome.

Study of the shape of the brain tells us that Pachycephalosaurus had an extremely good sense of smell, which probably helped it in looking for food or locating and fleeing from predators. The large orbits, protected dorsally by a bony ridge, and the development of the optic nerve in the brain also suggest that it had pretty good eyesight.

FINDING PACHYCEPHALOSAURUS FOSSILS

The story of the discovery of Pachycephalosaurus remains is rather complicated. A fragment of the skull dome was discovered as early as 1860, but it was not recognized as such. Paleontologist Ferdinand V. Hayden found it in southern Montana, and his colleague Joseph Leidy identified it as a piece of the armor of a reptile or an animal similar to an armadillo.

More fragmentary remains were discovered around 1930 and called Troodon wyomingensis, because they resembled another dinosaur named Troodon found by Hayden in Montana and studied by Leidy in 1856. It was then discovered that these belonged to a small carnivore, and today the name Troodon is attributed to a theropod dinosaur.

Left: A Pachycephalosaurus skull on exhibit in the Oxford University Museum of Natural History, Great Britain.

Above: A reconstruction of Pachycephalosaurus

Finally in 1940, a large almost complete skull was found north of Ekalaka in Montana. It was studied in 1943 by Barnum Brown and Erich M. Schlajker, who called it Pachycephalosaurus.

In recent years new forms of pachycephalosaurians have been discovered in the United States, but Pachycephalosaurus continues to be a rare animal. So far the remains of at least four skulls of this dinosaur have been found. An almost complete skull is on exhibit in the American Museum of Natural History in New York.

● Homalocephale,
Mongolia and China,
70.5–68.5 million years ago

● Prenocephale,
Mongolia,
70.5–68.5 million years ago

PACHYCEPHALOSAURIANS

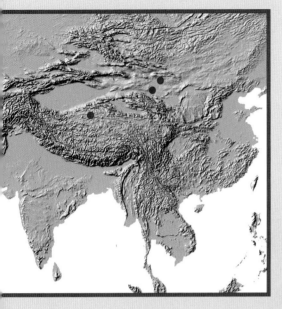

The maps show discovery sites
of the pachycephalosaurians
shown on these pages.

● Stegoceras,
United States and Canada,
76.5–75 million years ago

● Pachycephalosaurus,
United States and Canada,
67–65.5 million years ago

THE GREAT EXTINCTION

Sixty-five million years ago (about the time of Pachycephalosaurus), dinosaurs became extinct. Scientists think a large meteorite hitting the earth caused this extinction. A wide crater caused by a meteorite exactly 65 million years ago has been located along the coast of Mexico. The dust suspended in the air by the impact would have obscured the sunlight for a long time, causing a drastic drop in temperature and killing many plants.

The plant-eating dinosaurs would have starved or frozen to death. Meat-eating dinosaurs would have also died without their food supply. However, some scientists believe dinosaurs did not die out completely, and that present-day chickens and other birds are, in a way, the descendants of the large dinosaurs.

A DINOSAUR'S FAMILY TREE

The oldest dinosaur fossils are 220–225 million years old and have been found all over the world.

Dinosaurs are divided into two groups. Saurischians are similar to reptiles, with the pubic bone directed forward, while the Ornithischians are like birds, with the pubic bone directed backward.

Saurischians are subdivided in two main groups: Sauropodomorphs, to which quadrupeds and vegetarians belong; and Theropods, which include bipeds and predators.

Ornithischians are subdivided into three large groups: Thyreophorans which include the quadrupeds Stegosaurians and Ankylosaurians; Ornithopods; and Marginocephalians subdivided into the bipedal Pachycephalosaurians and the mainly quadrupedal Ceratopsians.

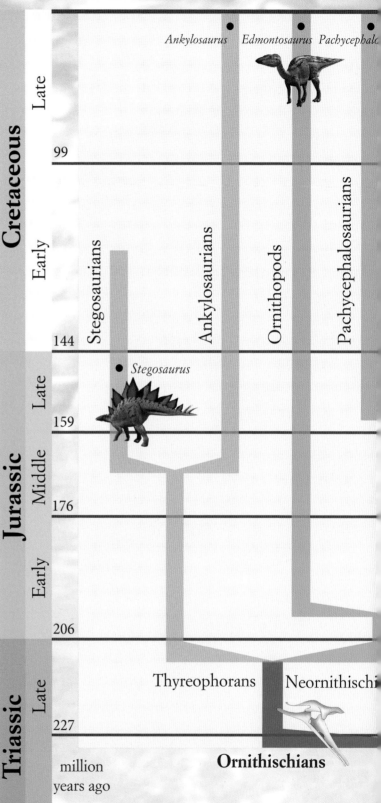

Ankylosaurus   Edmontosaurus   Pachycephalo...

Stegosaurians

Ankylosaurians

Ornithopods

Pachycephalosaurians

• *Stegosaurus*

Thyreophorans   Neornithischi...

Ornithischians

Cretaceous	Late	
		99
	Early	
		144
Jurassic	Late	
		159
	Middle	
		176
	Early	
		206
Triassic	Late	
		227

million years ago

26

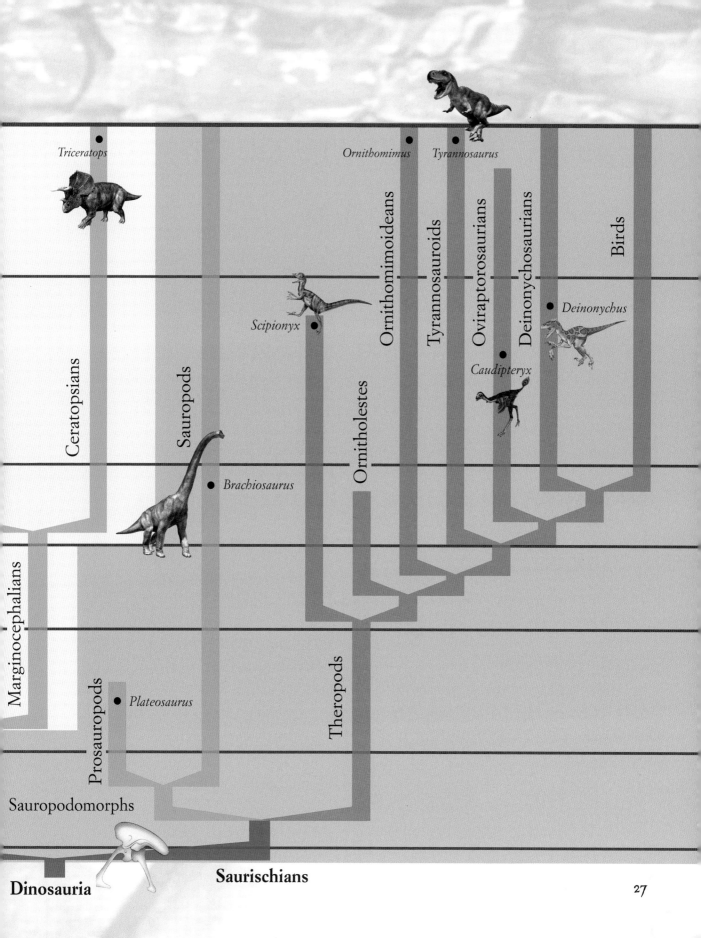

Triceratops

Ornithomimus

Tyrannosaurus

Ceratopsians

Ornithomimoideans

Tyrannosauroids

Oviraptorosaurians

Deinonychosaurians

Birds

Scipionyx

Deinonychus

Caudipteryx

Sauropods

Ornitholestes

Brachiosaurus

Marginocephalians

Theropods

Prosauropods

Plateosaurus

Sauropodomorphs

Dinosauria

Saurischians

A SHORT VOCABULARY OF DINOSAURS

Bipedal: pertaining to an animal moving on two feet alone, almost always those of the hind legs.

Bone: hard tissue made mainly of calcium phosphate; single element of the skeleton.

Carnivore: a meat-eating animal.

Caudal: pertaining to the tail.

Cenozoic Era (Caenozoic, Tertiary Era): the interval of geological time between 65 million years ago and present day.

Cervical: pertaining to the neck.

Claws: the fingers and toes of predator animals end with pointed and sharp nails, called claws. Those of plant-eaters end with blunt nails, called hooves.

Cretaceous Period: the interval of geological time between 144 and 65 million years ago.

Egg: a large cell enclosed in a porous shell produced by reptiles and birds to reproduce themselves.

Epoch: a division of geologic time.

Evolution: changes in the character states of organisms, species and higher ranks through time.

Feathers: outgrowth of the skin of birds and some other dinosaurs, used in flight and in providing insulation and protection of the body. They evolved from reptilian scales.

Forage: to wander in search of food.

Fossil: evidence of the life in the past. Not only bones, but footprints and trails made by animals, as well as dung, eggs, or plant resin, when fossilized, is a fossil.

Herbivore: a plant-eating animal.

Jurassic Period: the interval of geological time between 206 and 144 million years ago.

Mesozoic Era (Mesozoic, Secondary Era): the interval of the geological time between 248 and 65 million years ago.

Pack: a group of predator animals acting together to capture the prey.

Paleontologist: scientists who study and reconstruct prehistoric life.

Paleozoic Era (Paleozoic, Primary Era): the interval of geological time between 570 and 248 million years ago.

Predator: an animal that preys on other animals for food.

Raptor (raptorial): a bird of prey, such as an eagle, hawk, falcon, or owl.

Rectrix (plural rectrices): any of the larger feathers in a bird's tail that are important in helping its flight direction.

Scavenger: an animal that eats dead animals.

Skeleton: a structure of animal body made of several different bones. One primary function is also to protect delicate organs such as the brain, lungs, and heart.

Skin: the external, thin layer of the animal body. Skin cannot fossilize unless it is covered by scales, feathers, or fur.

Skull: bones that protect the brain and the face.

Teeth: tough structures in the jaws used to hold, cut, and sometimes process food.

Terrestrial: living on land.

Triassic Period: the interval of geological time between 248 and 206 million years ago.

Vertebrae: the single bones of the backbone; they protect the spinal cord.

DINOSAUR WEBSITES

Dinosaur Train (pbskids.com/dinosaurtrain/): From the PBS show Dinosaur Train, you can have fun watching videos, printing out pages to color, play games, and learn lots of facts about so many dinosaurs!

The Natural History Museum (http://www.nhm.ac.uk/kids-only/dinosaurs/): Take a quiz to see how much you know about dinosaurs or a quiz to tell you what type of dinosaur you'd be! There's also a fun directory of dinosaurs, including some cool 3D views of your favorites.

Discovery Channel Dinosaur videos (http://dsc.discovery.com/video-topics/other/dinosaur-videos): Watch almost 100 videos about the life of dinosaurs!

Dinosaurs for Kids (www.kidsdinos.com): There's basic information about most dinosaur types, and you can play dinosaur games, vote for your favorite dinosaur, and learn about the study of dinosaurs, paleontology.

DinoData (www.dinodata.org): Get the latest news on dinosaur research and discoveries. This site is pretty advanced, so you may need a teacher's or parent's help to find what you're looking for.

MUSEUMS

Yale Peabody Museum of Natural History, 170 Whitney Avenue, New Haven, CT 06520-8118

American Museum Natural History, Central Park West at 79th Street, New York, NY 10024-5192

The Field Museum, 1400 So. Lake Shore Drive, Chicago, IL 60605-2496

Carnegie Museum of Natural History, 4400 Forbes Avenue, Pittsburgh, PA 15213-4080

National Museum of Natural History, the Smithsonian Institution, 10th Street and Constitution Avenue NW, Washington, DC 20560-0136

Museum of the Rockies, 600 W. Kagy Boulevard., Bozeman, MT 59717

Denver Museum of Nature and Science, 2001 Colorado Boulevard, Denver, CO 80205

Dinosaur National Monument, Highway 40, Dinosaur, CO 81610

Sam Noble Museum of Natural History, 2401 Chautauqua, Norman, OK 73072-7029

Museum of Paleontology, University of California, 1101 Valley Life Sciences Bldg, Berkeley, CA 94720-4780

Royal Tyrrell Museum of Palaeontology, Hwy 838, Drumheller, AB T0J 0Y0, Canada

INDEX

Page numbers in **boldface** are illustrations.

....